YOU'VE
GUAC
TO BE JOKING!
I LOVE AVOCADOS

For Johno, Liz, Dad and Mum,
thanks for the puns and for
putting up with them.

POP PRESS

CAT FAULKNER

YOU'VE GUAC TO BE JOKING! I LOVE AVOCADOS

PRE HASS TORIC
DINE HASS AURS

TYRANNOSAURHASS

AVOCADODO

STONE HENGE

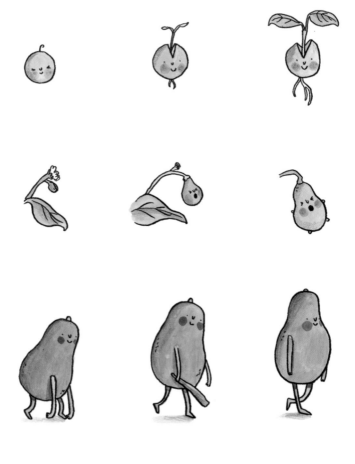

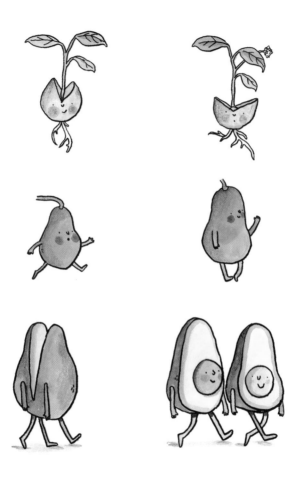

AVO-LUTION

AVOCADO TOAST

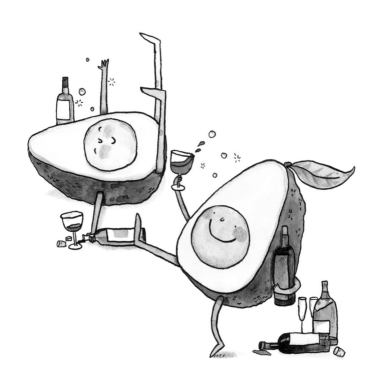

SMASHED AVOCADO

AVOCATDO

AVOCADOG

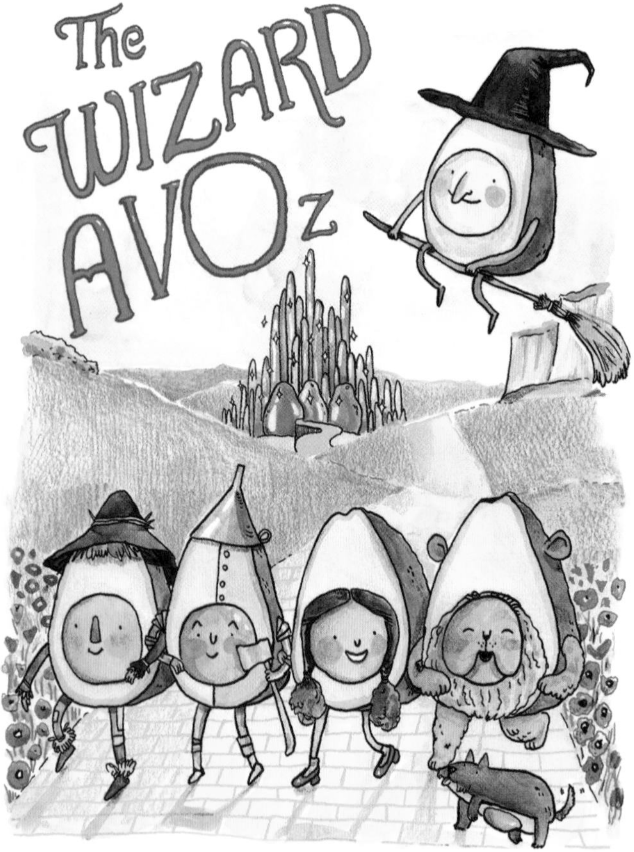
The WIZARD AVOz

Harry pitter

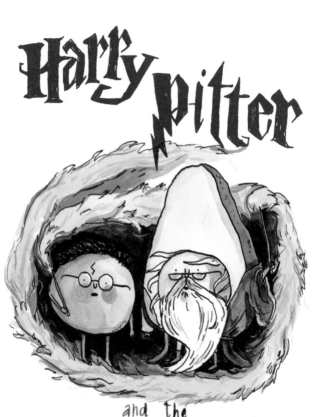

and the
Hass-Blood Prince

VINCENT VAN GUAC

PABLO PICAVO

GRIZZLY PEAR

HASS TEA RETREAT

THE HAPPY PEAR

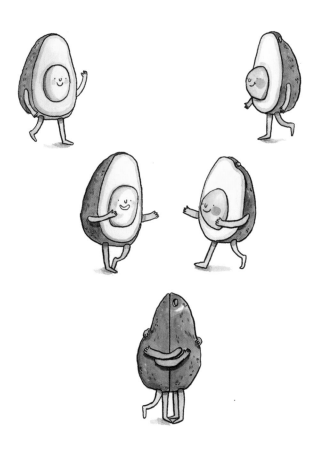

AVOCUDDLE

DOLLY PITON

DANCING GREEN

★AVVA★

HUGH GUACMAN IN

EGGS MEN

THOMHASS EDISON

HOVERCADO

ORCHESTRA PITS

NOAH'S AVOARKDO

AVOCADUCKS

AVOCADO RAP

GUACA MOLE

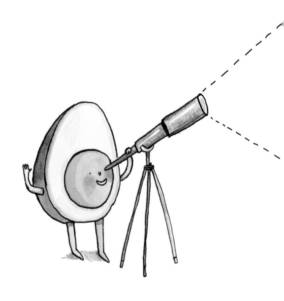

HASSTRONOMY

HASSTRONAUT

AVOCARPOOL

EMMA STONE

BRAD PIT

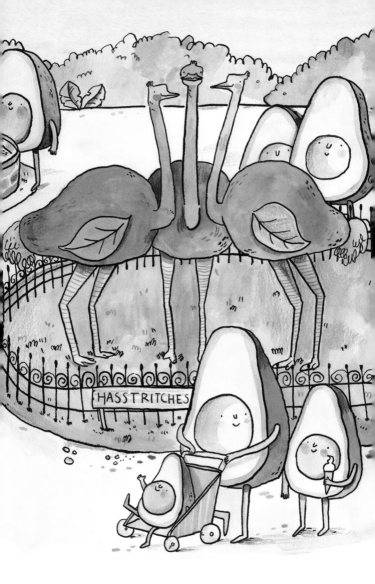

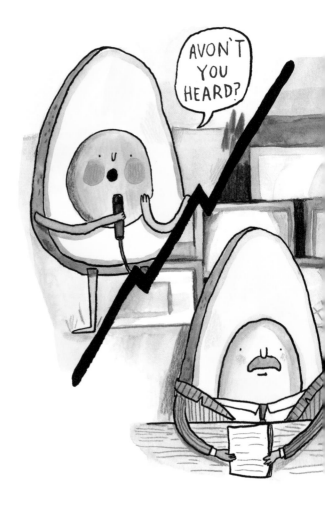

CRUSHED AVOCADO

THE LOVE GUACTOR

AVOTHA CHRISTIE

AVORIL LAVIGNE   PITNEY SPEARS

AVOCADO GRANDE

AVOCOWDO

PIT BULL

the CADO
on the RYE

ROLLING STONES

DAVID HASSLEHOFF

AVOCADO DIP

AVOCARPDO

AVOSHARKDO

STATUE OF LIBPITY

THE GUAC WALL OF CHINA

STONE COLD STEVE AUSTIN VS THE GUAC

I SEE YOU
BABY

SHAKING
THAT HASS

SHAKING
THAT HASS

SHAKING
THAT HASS

RIPE HERE, RIPE NOW, RIPE HERE
RIPE NOW, RIPE HERE, RIPE NOW
RIPE HERE, RIPE NOW, RIPE HERE
RIPE NOW, RIPE HERE, RIPE NOW
RIPE HERE, RIPE NOW, RIPE HERE
RIPE NOW, RIPE HERE, RIPE NOW
RIPE HERE
OW, RIPE HERE
RIPE NO
E, RIPE NOW
RIPE H
, RIPE HERE
RIPE N
, RIPE NOW
RIPE HE
RIPE HERE
RIPE NO
IPE NOW
RIPE HER
PE HERE
RIPE NOW,
, RIPE NOW
RIPE HERE,
OW, RIPE HERE

BRAVOCADO

AVOCANDOS

AVOCAN'T DOS

Guacula

Frankhasstein

HASS YOU LIKE IT

William Shakespear

The Pit of

Dorian Green

BRUCE SPRINGSGREEN

AVOCARDGAME

FIFTY SHADES
OF GREEN

PITTY WOMAN

THE LORD AVO THE RINGS

GAME of STONES

HE MAY BE SMALL & GREEN
BUT HE DOES AVOCADO

AVORAGE

AVOCADO ON
SOUR DOE

HASSABLANCA

BUTCH HASSIDY
AND THE
SUNDANCE PIT

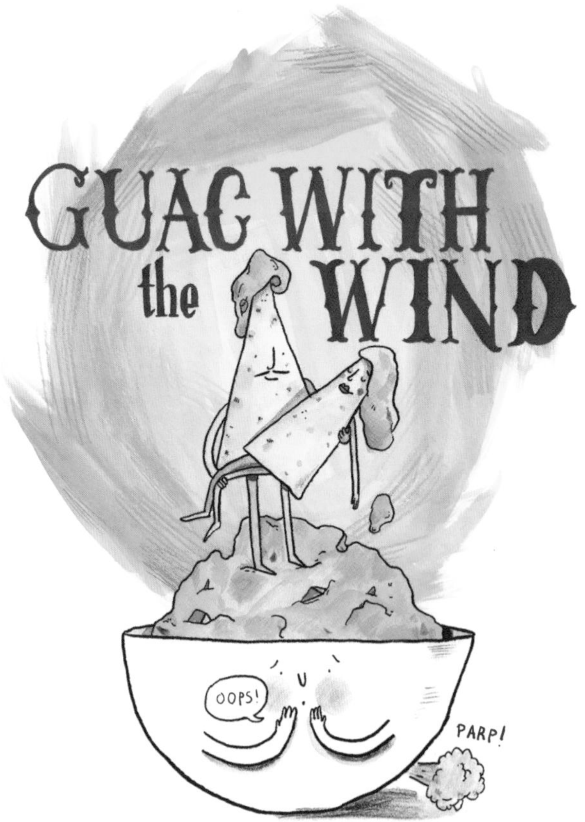
GUAC WITH the WIND
OOPS!
PARP!

GUAC HASSPECTATIONS

FRIDA KHAVO

AVO WARHOL

HASSASSINS

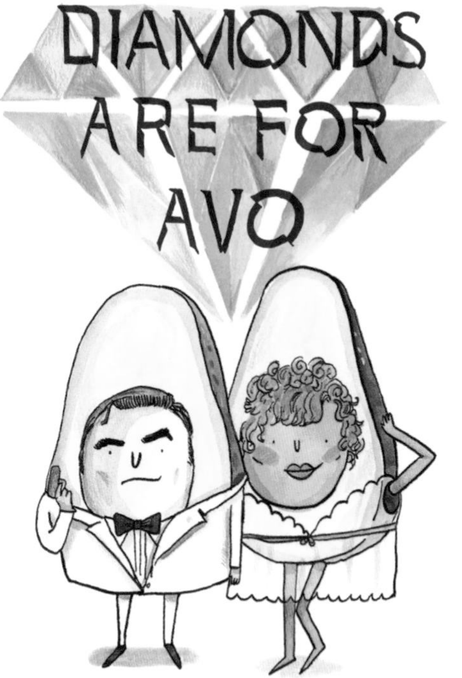
DIAMONDS
ARE FOR
AVO

BAD HASS

HASSTA LA VISTA
BABY

HOLY GUACAMOLE

DEVIL'S AVOCADO

THE GREEN MILE

BRIDGET STONE'S DIARY

AVODREY
HEPBURN

BRUNCH
AT TIFFANY'S

LOUIS PITTON   GUACCI

GUAC MARTENS   AVOCARGO
PANTS

MOUNT AVO REST

AVOLUNCH... AVOLANCHE... AVOLAUNCH

SEGREENA & VENHASS
WILLIAMS

AVOCARDIO

THE OLYMPITS

THE BIG DIPPER

JUPITER

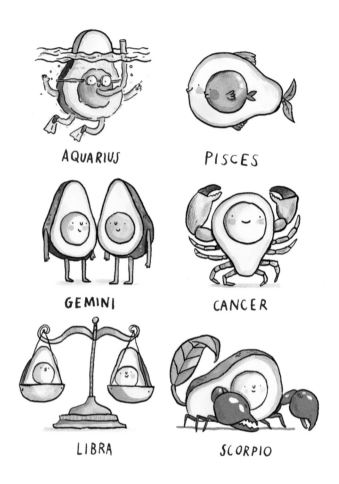

HASSTROLOGY

COLHASSEUM

THE ODHASSY

AMERICAN RIPE-O

CHILDREN OF THE AVO-LUTION

GuacAmore

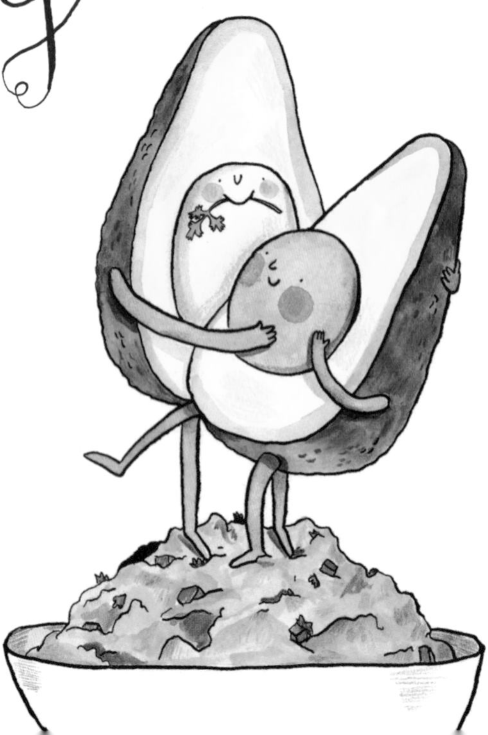

1 3 5 7 9 10 8 6 4 2

Pop Press, an imprint of Ebury Publishing,
20 Vauxhall Bridge Road,
London SW1V 2SA

Pop Press is part of the Penguin Random House
group of companies whose addresses can be
found at global.penguinrandomhouse.com

First published in the
United Kingdom by Pop Press in 2019

www.penguin.co.uk

A CIP catalogue record for this book is
available from the British Library

ISBN 9781785039362

Designed by Emily Voller
Printed and bound in China by Toppan Leefung
Colour origination by BORN Ltd

Penguin Random House is committed to a
sustainable future for our business, our readers
and our planet. This book is made from Forest
Stewardship Council® certified paper.

MIX
Paper from
responsible sources
FSC® C018179
www.fsc.org

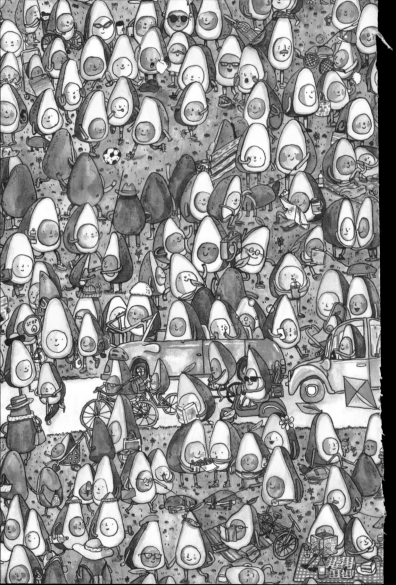